If You Give a Bunny a Beer

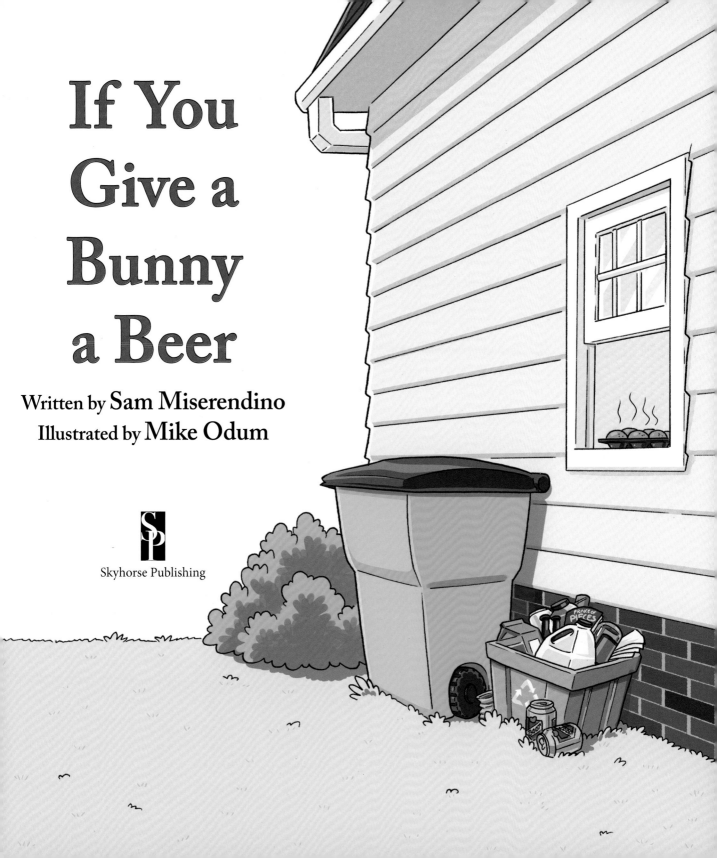

If You Give a Bunny a Beer

Written by **Sam Miserendino**
Illustrated by **Mike Odum**

Skyhorse Publishing

Skyhorse Publishing books may be purchased in bulk at special discounts for sales promotion, corporate gifts, fund-raising, or educational purposes. Special editions can also be created to specifications. For details, contact the Special Sales Department, Skyhorse Publishing, 307 West 36th Street,11th Floor, New York, NY 10018 or info@skyhorsepublishing.com.

Skyhorse® and Skyhorse Publishing® are registered trademarks of Skyhorse Publishing, Inc.®, a Delaware corporation.

Visit our website at www.skyhorsepublishing.com.

10 9 8 7 6

Library of Congress Cataloging-in-Publication Data is available on file

Cover and interior artwork by Mike Odum

Print ISBN: 978-1-5107-3395-4
eBook ISBN: 978-1-5107-3401-2

Printed in China

For Ariel and Sam
-S.M.

For Aurora
-M.O.

Special Thanks To:
Tosca Miserendino
Stacie Odum
Jeanne Miserendino
Beverly Miserendino

If you give a bunny a beer,

he'll want another.

And another…

And another…

And then he'll be sad, because it's not fun drinking alone.

SO...

He'll find some drinking buddies.

And they will be his
new best friends,

who understand him
better than anyone ever
has before.

When the beer
runs low...

He'll offer to make a beer run.

But he's not.

When he sees the doll's broken arm, it will remind him of his broken heart.

And he'll start to sob...

And sob...

And sob...

And how he lost her.

And he'll sob...

And sob...

Until, through
tears and beer goggles
he sees...

HER!

A vision of beauty
that makes him forget...

Whatever it was that he was crying about.

He'll woo her with poetry and wit.

He'll ask her
to dance.

He'll think he's moving like Michael Jackson...

But he's not.

When he bumps
into someone,

beer-brain
will make him
indignant.

And beer muscles will make him fearless.

When it's over,

he'll regret that he lost his temper. And regrets are like beer— one leads to another...

And another...   And another...

If only...

If only...

He had another beer!

Another beer will make
everything clear.

He'll tell you what's wrong
with the world.

He'll tell you
what's what.

And he'll tell you...

And tell you...

When he's finally
in bed,

the bed will
start spinning.

But he won't.

When he wakes up
the next morning,

he'll swear he absolutely, positively will never ever drink another beer in his life...

But he will.

The End

No bunnies were harmed
in the making of this book.
One did, however, have a
really good time.